Redeem Your F

Either scan the QR code

The Secrets Of Property Development
Live
by Samuel Leeds

Redeem Your FREE Ticket Here

Or visit:
www.property-investors.co.uk/development

The Secrets of Property Development

Samuel Leeds

Copyright 2021: Samuel Leeds
All rights reserved.
9798516788031

LEGAL NOTICES

The information presented herein represents the view of the authors as of the date of publication. Because of the rate with which conditions change, the author reserves the right to alter and update his opinion based on the new conditions. This book is for informational purposes only. While every attempt has been made to verify the information provided in this book, neither the authors nor their affiliates/partners assume any responsibility for errors, inaccuracies or omissions. Any slights of people or organisations are unintentional. You should be aware of any laws which govern business transactions or other business practices in your country and state. Any reference to any person or business whether living or dead is purely coincidental.

Every effort has been made to accurately represent this product and its potential but some sensitive information, such as people's names and addresses, may be changed for confidentiality reasons. Examples in these materials are not to be interpreted as a promise or guarantee of earnings. Earning potential is entirely dependent on the person using our product, ideas and techniques. We do not purport this as a "get rich scheme."

Your level of success in attaining the results claimed in our materials depends on the time you devote to the program, ideas and techniques mentioned your finances, knowledge and various skills. Since these factors differ according to individuals, we cannot guarantee your success or income level. Nor are we responsible for any of your Actions.

Any and all forward looking statements here or on any of our sales material are intended to express our opinion of earnings potential. Many factors will be important in determining your actual results and no guarantees are made that you will achieve results similar to ours or anybody else's, in fact no guarantees are made that you will achieve any results from our ideas and techniques in our material.

ALL RIGHTS RESERVED. No part of this course may be reproduced or transmitted in any form whatsoever, electronic, or mechanical, including photocopying, recording, or by any informational storage or retrieval without the expressed written consent of the authors.

Foreword by Liv Cooke..Pg11

CHAPTER 1 - My Target to Own 1,000 Houses Pg17

CHAPTER 2 - Billionaire Boardroom Session with
Lord Sugar..Pg21

CHAPTER 3 – Big Deals Are Easier Than Small Deals ...Pg27

CHAPTER 4 – Buying Land on Option Agreements.........Pg33

CHAPTER 5 - Finding Sites and Securing Deals.............Pg39

CHAPTER 6 - Declined Planning Permission Cost Me
A Fortune Pg43

CHAPTER 7 - The Profit Is In The Planning Pg47

CHAPTER 8 - Building Houses Just Makes Sense.........Pg55

CHAPTER 9 - Why I Lent Millions To Others Pg59

CHAPTER 10 - Avoiding The Classic Development Scam
....Pg63

CHAPTER 11 - Why I Bought A Castle...........................Pg67

CHAPTER 12 - Lessons From The Castle,
Ribbesford House..Pg81

CHAPTER 13 - How To Minimise Your Tax.....................Pg99

CHAPTER 14 - If You're So Rich, Why Borrow Other
People's Money?..Pg107

CHAPTER 15 - My Property Development Business
Plan Pg115

Exact Next Steps To Get Started..................................Pg124

Foreword by Liv Cooke

My name is Liv Cooke and some of you may know me as a former football freestyle world champion, and the holder of five world records. Others might know me more as a BBC sports presenter or perhaps for my growing social media platforms which have attracted more than seven million followers. I am also the co-founder of Winning Wealth LTD alongside my good friend and property legend Samuel Leeds, the author of this book.

I would like to tell you about why I started out on my own property journey and how that path led me to Samuel's door.

Back in 2016 when I was training for the world championships, which I would go on to win, I became obsessed with success and improving every day in every way. I studied leaders across all industries such as Floyd Mayweather, Ronda Rousey, Cristiano Ronaldo, Conor McGregor, Nicki Minaj and... Grant Cardone. Since you have picked up this book, I am going to assume you know that last name very well! Unintentionally, this was my first real exposure to the real estate industry.

Despite being massively interested in property investing back then, I did not take any further action for a while. My focus remained solely on my dream of becoming world champion. However, when I won my gold medal in 2017, I was finally able to open my vision up. I explored my passion for all things business and began building up my career to where it is today.

It was a rollercoaster of a journey packed with plenty of highs and lows, but fast forward to 2019 and I was earning what I considered to be a high amount of active income. I was a UEFA football ambassador, a presenter on a prime time television show and still growing rapidly on social media. I was, and still am, loving life! It was never about the money for me, it was all about becoming the best I could be, making a positive impact and enjoying every day as if it was my last. But, I was not naive. I knew that deals come and go, that there is no stability in the field I was in, and that I needed to take action to secure my financial future. And, thanks to my earlier research into successful people, I knew exactly how I was going to do that...

The following day I bought the top five recommended books for property investing and read them all within a week or two. I watched hundreds of property videos on YouTube and thousands of minutes of podcasts. I set up an Instagram account dedicated to property and went on to follow every rising star in the sector. A certain name kept popping up. He was absolutely everywhere. Yep, you guessed it... Samuel Leeds.

The more I looked into Samuel the more fascinated I became. He seemed to be the leading figure in the UK for all things property. Being a champion I knew the fastest way to learn and climb in a new industry is to find the leader and learn from them. I approached Samuel with the idea of offering him value – exposure in return for knowledge. I knew he was a busy guy so I didn't want to ask for much. Nervously, I dropped him a message asking if he had a spare ten minutes or so to jump on a video call with me. To my surprise he replied almost instantly with a yes. The next day we ended up chatting for more than an hour. He was extremely impressed with my level of knowledge and agreed to mentor me on my journey.

"Liv, I know who you are and you're a winner. I know that if you're serious about getting into property you're heading straight to the top. With your drive you'll succeed with or without me but I'd be honoured to help guide you on your journey."

Over time Samuel and I grew closer and closer. I shadowed him for days on end, documenting his journey from first visiting a site and analysing the numbers, all the way through to completing and executing on the exit strategy. I watched him do this time after time, taking it all in like a sponge.

In the process of mentoring me and guiding me as I built my own successful property portfolio, I got to know Samuel on a much deeper level. He visited me in Manchester many times, invited me to his house and introduced me to his family. I felt completely at home as Russell (Samuel's brother) spoke football to me, Amanda (Samuel's wife) offered me a drink and their little boy was kicking footballs around the garden.

The longer I spent with Samuel and the more I learnt about property, the more I fell in love with the industry. It started as a way to protect my financial future, but evolved into something much more than that. My inner champion took over and I became obsessed. I studied every aspect of the process, analysed every strategy and became a very competent investor.

I had so many people messaging me and asking for advice, including many celebrities. However, I did not feel confident enough to offer direct advice and allow them to risk their resources on my opinion. So I would offer my thoughts and explain what I would do in their situation, but then kindly recommend they speak to Samuel to see if he agreed. And, he did. Every single time in fact and as a result my confidence rocketed. Fast forward to 2021 and we are executing on this weekly.

Samuel is an incredible mentor and we get on so well. He really believed in me when no-one else did and guided me during my early days. He is one of only a few people in the world to actively and openly share their secrets of success.

His passion is admirable, his work ethic unmatchable and his heart incredible. Words cannot do this man justice. I am proud to not only have been mentored by Samuel, but to have gone on to co-found 'Winning Wealth LTD' with him to help stars of today secure their financial futures.

I could talk forever about all the work we are doing together and all the wonderful things Samuel does for others, but I do not want to digress from this book's purpose too much. So, I will end on something Samuel said to me when I was starting out.

"Liv, don't buy from a developer, BE the developer!"

CHAPTER 1 - My Target to Own 1,000 Houses

When I was a kid I was pretty bad at most things. I was average at sports, unpopular with the girls and struggled with anything academic.

I was the middle child with an older brother and a younger sister. My brother Russell was excellent at most things. He was a whiz in school and everybody liked him. My dad praised him, but could not get over why I was not the same.

My sister, Tiffany, is drop-dead gorgeous and four years younger than me. She was the only girl and the baby of the family. I never fitted in anywhere I went, and all my life have felt misunderstood.

My parents got divorced when I was seven years old and later my mum married one of my schoolteachers. I hated school!

The one thing I loved doing was my paper round. I was extremely competitive and constantly challenging myself about how many papers I could deliver in an evening. I got paid about £17 to deliver 800 newspapers, but I could earn more by putting advertisement leaflets in the newspapers before I delivered them. The more newspapers and leaflets I could pop through letterboxes, the more money I would make. Let me tell you − I delivered one heck of a lot of papers!

At school I overheard my teachers complaining about how little they were paid and that they could not afford the things they wanted. Despite me not being very good in their classes and struggling with my homework, it was a strange but liberating feeling, knowing I had hundreds of pounds sitting in my Bradford and Bingley savings account.

On one occasion when I was about fourteen, I showed my teacher that I had £650 in my bank. She gasped and said: "That's more money than I've got!"

I did not mean to show off, I was just really proud of myself and felt such a strong sense of achievement. I had never been good at anything before, but I had finally found something I loved doing and was in complete control of – accumulating wealth!

This new-found hobby resulted in me becoming a big fan of Monopoly. I also started finding other ways to make money, such as washing cars and selling things to school mates.

When I was delivering papers to the small terraced houses around Walsall, I used to dream of owning the houses. Whilst this excitement for wealth made school even more mundane, it also gave me the spark I was missing. My confidence started to take root.

I read Richard Branson's book 'Screw It, Let's Do It' and ironically, I became more interested in certain subjects at school including maths. I used to put £ symbols before the numbers to add a bit of spice. I ended up getting a B in my maths GCSE which was far better than my predicted E from my teacher. I overheard my step-dad tell somebody that watching me grow up was fascinating, almost like watching a mini-Richard Branson. This changed the whole way I perceived myself. I was no longer the stupid kid who was not good at anything, I was an entrepreneur!

I have often talked about my journey from leaving school to building up a large property portfolio from scratch in books and YouTube videos. I bought my first house in 2009 which was very creatively and financially structured to make it a "no money down deal."

In my early twenties I was constantly invited to share my story at business conferences on how I had become a property millionaire with dozens of houses at such a young age. I was playing Monopoly in real life and my goal was to own 1,000 houses whilst still in my thirties. By the age of 26, in 2017, my portfolio was snowballing and I was winning big.

CHAPTER 2 - Billionaire Boardroom Session with Lord Sugar

My plans of owning 1,000 properties was always applauded by my mentors and peers. I had also become very popular in the media as I symbolised youthful entrepreneurialism. I was approached by many people from all walks of life who wanted to pat me on the back and pick my brain.

Within a matter of months of finding a new mentor, I would become richer than they were. My portfolio was rising in value and I was leveraging the equity to buy more and more houses.

As a by-product of finding good property deals for myself, I was packaging and selling hundreds of property investment deals and using the money to expand my portfolio.

Every time I had a strategy session with my mentor, I would far surpass the targets that were set. I spent a small fortune on hiring new coaches who could help me to raise the bar even higher. It was a struggle to find people who were more successful than I was, or whom I would not overtake very quickly. That changed when I received an invitation to attend a business conference where Lord Sugar would be speaking.

I thought it would be a good idea to attend as I had never met Lord Sugar and he was a billionaire who held most of his wealth in real estate. Before booking tickets, I rang up the event organisers and explained that I really wanted an opportunity to sit down with Lord Sugar and get some bespoke guidance on my business plan to own 1,000 homes.

To my surprise, they said yes. So long as I paid £4,800, I would be able to sit around a table for at least an hour with only five other business owners, and ask Lord Sugar any personal questions I had relevant to my business. I immediately paid the money as I thought this was a rare opportunity that could prove priceless. Afterall I thought he must know something more than I do because his bank balance is even bigger than mine!

So, on November 10th, 2017, I found myself sitting around a private boardroom table with Lord Sugar at the Heathrow Airport Hilton Hotel, confidently ready to present my business plan.

I was a little nervous because I had seen him on TV so many times, ruthlessly ripping people to shreds in boardrooms, but this was different. I had a solid business plan, I was rapidly making money and my property portfolio was booming.

Lord Sugar picked up his pen, looked me straight in the eye and said,

"Tell me about your business."

I did not see this as a case of me pitching to him or trying to impress him. It was simply my chance to see how I could tweak, improve, or fast-track my goal of owning 1,000 properties.

I explained where I was as an entrepreneur.

"I'm in the real estate business. I already have a million-pound portfolio of residential properties, mostly consisting of single-family homes and HMOs. I'm making a minimum of £10,000 per month packaging and selling property investments to other investors, and using this money to put down more deposits on properties to scale up my portfolio. My target is to own 1,000 houses."

I was waiting for Lord Sugar to pat me on the back and tell me how well I'd done for a 26-year-old. Oh, how wrong I was! He pulled a face as if he had just swigged a bottle of vinegar or sucked a bag of lemons!

"Why on earth would you want to do that?"

I was shocked. I could not believe he was saying this when he himself was a property billionaire. I assumed he must be talking about the deal packaging I had mentioned. Maybe he did not like the idea of selling deals to other investors. I began to explain how deal sourcing worked and how much money I was making by providing a service for investors who did not have the time or inclination to find their own investments.

He looked over my plans and said that the deal sourcing 'made sense.' He seemed relatively impressed with that side of things, but he could not get over the idea of me wanting to own 1,000 homes.

"Owning a thousand houses means owning a thousand boilers too," he said. "What are you going to do when they keep breaking down and the tenants keep on calling you? I can't imagine it would be very profitable."

Unfazed, I showed him my profit margins and explained

how my HMO properties made enough profit to cover maintenance. I outlined my power team, how the whole process was systemised and how this led to good profit margins. He seemed to warm to me as a person, but he remained cool on the idea of owning so many properties. He kept emphasising how big a headache it would be and that there were far better ways to invest in real estate.

This was a really hard pill to swallow as I was so focused and determined to continue to scale my portfolio as I had been doing. However, I decided not to argue and just listen. Lord Sugar was not being a jerk, or acting provocatively for the sake of it. He was just trying to help me. There were no video cameras or a TV audience in the room. He was speaking from experience and he knew far more than I did about being a property billionaire.

Lord Sugar made me realise that my target of owning so many houses was more of an ego thing. I just wanted to be able to say it as it had a great ring to it. But really, any smart businessperson will tell you that the target in business should be simply to make as much profit as possible. The goal should not be to own as many houses as possible, but to make as much money as possible. Property was the vehicle to generate profit, not the other way around.

I learnt that day that nearly every property billionaire, invests in big deals. You have to scale up and increase the *size* of your deals, not the number of them. I have never met anybody who owns more than 100 houses who is also a smart businessperson. Small deals require just as much effort and work as big deals, but big deals make far more profit.
The thing that makes you financially comfortable is not the

thing that makes you a millionaire. And the thing that makes you a millionaire is not the thing that makes you a billionaire. I now needed to stop what I was doing and start playing a new game.

Lord Sugar had shattered my business plan, but had handed me a new Monopoly board.

CHAPTER 3 - Big Deals Are Easier Than Small Deals

At the back end of 2017, I made a decision to concentrate solely on bigger deals. It was suddenly all so obvious. All my heroes in business were focusing on building skyscrapers and housing estates, not buying single residential homes. If I was to make £250,000 profit per property deal, I would need to do fewer deals but ones which made a lot more money.

I started to talk to friends who were doing major deals and began to put out feelers for larger projects that I could sink my teeth into. I put in a few offers on some meaty pub conversions and some run down office blocks, but this was all new territory for me.

I had conversations with agents about plots of land with development potential and it felt like starting over again. I began to notice that landlords with huge portfolios were much busier and nowhere near as wealthy as more sophisticated developers.

For me, transitioning into bigger development deals was the logical next step. Doing small deals forever would be no different than trying to become a millionaire through delivering more papers. That would have been an insane aim requiring an immense amount of hard work. Billionaires do not necessarily work harder than millionaires, they just do different things. If you are going to work hard anyway, you might as well get very rich by working smarter.

Lord Robert Edmiston was a self-made billionaire who acted as a mentor to me on The Lions UK – a Christian training programme for entrepreneurs and pioneers.

I have always admired the way Bob (as he was known to friends and associates) gave away vast amounts to charity. He and his son Andrew made tens of millions of pounds in profits every year through property development in the UK. Their company owned almost half of Solihull shopping centre, and they were building large luxury housing estates. I informally started picking their brains on property and soon realised that their business model was far superior to what I had been planning.

Andrew was extremely generous with his knowledge and time, and we connected regularly through church and charity. He could see that although I was ambitious to make money, I was ultimately doing it to leave a legacy and help make a difference in the world, not just live a life of idle luxury.

I was invited to spend a week with Andrew at his stunning ski chalet in Avoriaz, in the French Alps. I had been there the year before and had loved it, not just for the skiing and the scenery but also the great company.

Andrew would invite two or three other people and we would spend time chewing the fat. We chatted a bit about business, but mainly about our charitable aims and next steps.

Could Andrew be my property mentor? It seemed so obvious. The only problem was that he was a friend through church. We were mostly there to relax and advance our charitable causes and I did not want to corner him into spending hours talking about my personal business plans.

I was determined not to overstep the mark, particularly as Andrew would never charge me for business mentorship. He was more than happy to help as a favour. However, in my experience, when you are not paying for advice, it is near impossible to get proper guidance. So I took the opportunity when we had a small gap in our skiing schedule to tell Andrew about a deal I was about to sign, as part of a partnership. He asked to see the bullet points of the agreement.

After studying the details, he strongly advised me not to sign it.

It was a big deal which I was very excited about. I told him I really wanted to go ahead and time was of the essence.

"Let's talk about it tomorrow after skiing and I'll have a proper look at the deal and the contracts," he said.

All day while skiing I just wanted to talk about it. I wanted to know how I could have negotiated it better. I was worried that if I delayed too much the deal could fall out of bed. Andrew told me to relax and enjoy the skiing.

During dinner later that evening I was desperate to go over the details, but again I did not want to be a pain to him. Andrew had not invited me so that I could rinse his knowledge all week. He was also kindly letting let me stay in his luxury chalet for free.

At 9pm that day, Andrew asked me to email him the particulars of the deal, which I immediately did. He disappeared for half an hour and then came back with a very creative new agreement with several amended terms.

The deal in question was quite complicated and confidential, so I cannot go into the fine details, but I studied his suggestions in an increasing state of shock and admiration.

"Andrew, if this comes off it will literally make me an additional £1,600,000!"

"It will come off," he replied. "Get on the phone now and make it happen."

It took a few weeks for the deal to be finalised. I did not make £1,600,000 in cash right away, but as a result of that 30-minute mentorship I am almost £2,000,000 richer at the time of writing.

Andrew now jokingly tells me that I owe him a handsome commission, but in all seriousness I am so grateful to him for his informal mentorship and guidance. Often it only takes a billionaire a few minutes to change the course of another person's life. Most people reinvent the wheel and try to become successful alone, whereas wise people learn from other people's vast experience and mistakes.

Most people work 40 hours per week for 40 years and get paid £40,000… if they are lucky! This means that a well-paid job will earn you £1,600,000 over your entire lifetime. Andrew Edmiston spent 30 minutes looking over a deal, which made me more money than most people earn in a lifetime.

Lord Sugar does not even remember giving me any business advice and later told The Sun newspaper that he had never heard of me. Whilst this did surprise and offend me a little at the time, I am still eternally grateful for his rich words of wisdom.

Lord Edmiston gave up a few evenings to train and mentor me and a small group of other entrepreneurs, and it turned out to be life changing for me.

I now felt like king of the world and was ready for my next big deal. It takes just as much energy to make £10,000 as it does to make £1,000,000.

CHAPTER 4 - Buying Land on Option Agreements

Over the last ten years, I have become an expert at buying ordinary three-bed terraced houses, and massively increasing their values by changing their use from a single-family home to a House in Multiple Occupation (HMO).

I bought my first house in Birmingham for £100,000 which was well below market value. I turned the place into an HMO and immediately refinanced it to its true, higher value of £120,000. This enabled me to get a new mortgage of £100,000 which was 100% of my investment back. I have since done similar deals hundreds of times either for myself or my clients.

My brother, Russell, was really behind my idea of targeting bigger projects and was excited about my new change in direction. He himself had just completed on a development deal in partnership with our step-dad, Tim, where he had turned a large Victorian house in Market Drayton into a block of flats. He paid £120,000 for the property, spent £30,000 on planning and conversion, and increased the value to £220,000. Whilst this was a little bigger than the properties I was usually doing, it still was not something I could imagine a billionaire doing. I needed something even bigger.

I had a voicemail from an estate agent in Derby saying there was an off-market piece of land I might be interested in. I was excited and immediately requested more information. The estate agent totally understood what I was looking to do, and we connected really well.

The land was on offer for £100,000 and had the potential

to house five new apartments. I went to the site to have a look and to talk to David, the agent.

The problem was that I did not really know what I was looking for. I had no idea how much it would cost to build five apartments in Derby, as I had never done it before. David said it was supposed to be going to market the following Monday, but I wanted first dibs on the deal.

I did not feel it was appropriate for me to call Andrew or Bob, and I had not got an official mentor in the property development space, so I just called a few acquaintances who I knew had more experience than me. I was wary of revealing the exact details of the site in case anyone tried to steal it from me, so I only spoke to people I knew I could trust.

Looking at the end values of similar new-build apartments, it seemed they would be worth about £175,000 each once finished. That would represent a total Gross Development Value (GDV) of £875,000.

David, the agent, had CGIs (computer-generated imagery) showing exactly what the apartments would look like once finished and where they would be built on the site. He was very confident that planning permission would be granted and that their value would be at least £875,000.

Russell suggested that I check what other new-builds within 0.5 miles of the site had recently sold for. After comparing their square footage with mine I was very sure of my end value estimate. I spoke to three other estate agents in the area who had recently sold new apartments and they all confirmed my estimate was realistic.

I was feeling pretty excited about my first potential development site because I was confident that it would not cost more than about £400,000 to build the entire block. I knew many builders from my years in the industry and asked them for their professional opinions. Each confirmed that £400,000 would be reasonable to build all five apartments and that there was plenty of space on the site to do so comfortably at that price.

What else could I be missing? The land was located in a desirable part of Derby and the figures seemed to be stacking up. I knew that I would need an architect, a structural engineer, a quantity surveyor and potentially other professionals to pull off a development like this. I had never done anything like this before and I was excited at the prospect of a new challenge.

My predictions:

Purchase price for the land: £100,000
Gross Development Cost including professional fees: £450,000
Gross Development Value: £875,000

This meant that if I bought the land, I could hand it over to the building team and other professionals to make a clean profit of £325,000! There would be a small amount of tax to pay the council (by virtue of Section 106 of the Planning Act 2008 and/or the Community Infrastructure Levy (normally referred to as CIL), but that would only be around £6,000.

David called me and asked me what I wanted to do. I had already shown him my proof of funds, so he knew I was serious and he was familiar with me because we had some mutual connections. I told him I was really keen to go ahead but still needed confirmation that I would be granted planning permission to build the apartments. He advised me to speak to the council but stressed I would have to act quickly as the land would need to go to market within a matter of days.

I rang the council and asked them about the site in question and they told me to submit a pre-planning application which would tell me whether it would be permitted or not. They advised this could be a four to six-week process. I did not have time to wait for this as it would put me at risk of losing the site. Even if the seller was not in a rush, if I managed to get planning permission to build the site, it would dramatically increase in value.

While pondering what to do, I decided to go for a walk and think. I came up with a completely genius idea – even if I say so myself! I crafted an agreement that I thought would revolutionise the way that property development is done and make me millions. The concept was very similar to how I had purchased small residential homes many times over. It was a 'lease option agreement.'

What if I were to offer the seller £110,000, which is £10,000 more than he wanted, but in 12 months' time? This would give me a year to get planning permission. I could then simply assign the option to a new buyer and keep the difference. This is how I envisaged the agreement to look:

> Stage 1: Agree an Option Agreement giving me the option to purchase the land in 12 months for £110,000. I would get a solicitor to draw up the agreement to ensure it was legally watertight.

Stage 2: Apply for and obtain planning permission and have time to carry out all groundwork at a very small cost. If planning were refused, I would just walk away losing very little.

Stage 3: Once planning permission was granted to build the five apartments I would simply assign the option to somebody else at a much higher price – e.g. £200,000.

This would leave the new buyer with no risks to worry about because planning permission was already in place. Basically the profit hinged purely on gaining planning permission. The buyer would still make a decent amount from building the apartments while I would actually be doing very little!

I spoke to some agents about the land. They confirmed that once planning permission was in place, it should easily sell for between £200,000 and £250,000. If I could pull this off, I would make about £100,000 profit within less than 12 months and would not even have ever owned anything. I would not have to build anything either. I would just be securing sites on an option, gaining planning permission and assigning them to somebody else for a profit. Now you know what I mean by genius!

CHAPTER 5 - Finding Sites and Securing Deals

I texted David at 9:07pm on a Friday evening.

I said: I have a formal offer for the land in Derby, can we speak?"

I frantically waited for David to respond, but all I got was silence.

I was excited, but also anxious that somebody else could come in and offer to buy the plot over the weekend. I thought it might seem too desperate ringing him late at night, so decided to wait until the morning.

I spent all night searching for land. I was looking at stuff on the market but also using Google Earth to find sites with development potential. I drafted a new letter to send to landowners.

It read:

> Dear (name),
>
> I can see that you are the owner of some land located in (street and town name). I am a property developer and would be interested in having an informal conversation to explore possibilities of buying the land from you.
>
> If you are open to selling or developing, please contact me either by text or email.
>
> Kind Regards,

Samuel Leeds
07*********
samuel@*******.com

I knew that having multiple potential deals on the table would put me in the strongest position to negotiate. Desperation is the worst emotion to have during any kind of negotiation, and I was beginning to feel a little too emotionally invested in the Derby site. There was so much land around it was difficult to know where to start. I began looking in places where I already owned houses and knew the areas well. There are many quick and easy ways to discover who owns a piece of land especially if owned by a company, but in the worst case scenario you can just pay £3 to the Land Registry and find the owner of any given site.

I waited a painfully long two days to hear back from David, who said he would speak to the seller and come back to me. In my experience, agents never explain lease options very well to sellers, and I was concerned that he would do a bad job of pitching the idea.

I told David that I would prefer to talk to the seller direct, to which he agreed hesitantly and insisted he should be in on the call too. That same Monday afternoon we had a three-way telephone call. I felt I had pitched the concept so beautifully I was convinced the landowner would say yes:

> "You want £100,000 for the land and you don't want any hassle. You aren't in a rush for the money but don't want to develop it yourself. Is this correct?"

"Basically, yes. That is right," the seller confirmed.

"Well," I said, "I may be able to offer something like this. I could give you £110,000 for the land which is 10% higher than what you are asking for. The only thing I will need in return is a maximum of 12 months to sort out the planning permission to build. How does that sound?"

"What if I just want the money now?" he responded.

It was time for some straight talking:

"Currently the site is not worth much at all because there is no planning permission, so it is just a worthless piece of earth. "Right now I couldn't give you more than £50,000 cash for the land."

My good friend and architect, David Taylor, is known for saying that land without planning is only worth as much as an expensive piece of carpet. Amazingly, this is a great way to value land without planning permission.

The seller was very offended at my £50,000 offer and said he would think about my Lease Option proposal. David said he was going to put the property on the market and see what other buyers had to say. I came off the call feeling pretty deflated. I had spent so much time thinking about this wretched piece of land and it was looking increasingly unlikely it was going to come off.

David called me later that day and said,

"I think I could persuade the seller to go with your

proposal, but I have got other buyers interested now. If I get this wrapped up for you as a lease option, I really want a £5,000 fee for my efforts. What do you reckon?"

I thought David was a little cheeky here because in my opinion he should not end up being paid by both parties on the deal, but I was not going to cause a fuss. He was a one-man band agency and if he could get me that deal on an option, it was probably worth the £5,000 fee as I was set to make 20x that on the deal itself. I agreed.

On the Tuesday afternoon I received a call from David, saying the seller had agreed but wanted a £10,000 non-refundable deposit. That way, he would still get £110,000, but if I did not buy it at the end of the 12 months I would have to lose the £10,000. I actually thought this was fair and we shook hands on the deal. The legals were drawn up and I was over the moon! The day the contacts were signed felt like a dream come true for me, but it very quickly turned into a living nightmare!

CHAPTER 6 - Declined Planning Permission Cost Me A Fortune

I embarked on a steep learning curve soon after taking control of that piece of land in Derby on an option agreement. I was already £16,500 down because I had paid a £10,000 option fee to the seller, a £5,000 finder's fee to David and £1,500 on the legal paperwork.

The drawings David had provided me with looked very glamorous, but they were quite basic and I received conflicting advice from everybody I spoke to. It became clear that the CGIs were more geared to a sales brochure than anything we could realistically submit in our planning application. I had a Premier League power team for property investing, but my property development squad would have struggled in League Two. It turned out that the builders I had been talking to, did not have a clue about planning permission and neither did I. David had disappeared from the face of the earth and I did not have a planning consultant to turn to. I was out of my depth and in need of urgent help.

I rang a friend of mine who had a property development training company and appeared to know about development. I will refer to him as Kevin as I would rather not reveal his true identity. 'Kevin' told me that if I played my cards right, I could still make this Derby site profitable, but it was going to be difficult to get planning permission for five apartments because it was not in keeping with the area.

The proposed size of the apartment block would overshadow the neighbours' views. I began to get a little worried and was a tad embarrassed that I had got myself into such a pickle. I asked him if he wanted to take half of the profits and just come in with me on the deal. Kevin said he would come on board as a development mentor for £10,000 and help me make it work. After some negotiation, we agreed £5,000 upfront and then £5,000 if the site managed to make more than £75,000 profit. I doubted Kevin a little because if he believed in the site, surely he would want to be a 50/50 partner. Why would he only want £10,000 when the dividends could be so much greater? But I was in a spot and wanted his help.

Kevin turned out to be as useful as a chocolate fireguard. He took £5,000 from me, but did not have the first clue about development. He was just a polished salesman who could talk the talk.

After applying for planning permission, it turned out that the site was suitable, but it was in a high flood risk area. That was something that never came up with the solicitors as it was only an option agreement. They do not carry out that kind of due diligence for option agreements – that was the job of the developer – me!

In hindsight, I feel very stupid for not checking the flood risk of the site. It would have taken me less than a minute to have gone onto the government website, typed in the address and seen that in was in a 'high flood risk zone.' This would have immediately been a massive red flag to me. I would have walked away from a lot of stress and the loss of £30,000!

Me being me, I still tried to make the deal work and paid a flood risk assessor to try to help the situation, but with the associated costs and insurance needed, it just was not viable.

I was so angry with David and Kevin and felt like I had been stitched up like a kipper. No wonder the seller had wanted a £10,000 non-refundable fee. Surely, he must have suspected that I would have no chance of getting planning permission? As disappointed as I was with everybody else, I was mostly disappointed with myself. I had to take full responsibility and get better rather than bitter. I realised I needed a full checklist of what to look for in a development opportunity. I vowed never again to let my emotions get the better of me in this more complex level of the game. I had gained something from the experience though - I had learnt an extremely valuable lesson.

CHAPTER 7 - The Profit Is In The Planning

The reason I lost money on the Derby deal was simply because I did not know what I was doing. I decided to stop sending letters to landowners and hold off speaking to any more agents. I needed to educate myself. I was already well acquainted with valuing property, negotiating deals and being creative with purchasing no-money-down deals such as lease options. Now I had to master the rules of planning permission and appraising development sites.

I began by studying the Strategic Housing and Economic Land Availability Assessment (SHELAA) which is freely available on the government website. I was blown away at how much information is made public, even to the extent of local authorities highlighting specific pieces of land that would be suitable for development! I always knew that there was a shortage of houses in the UK, but I was unaware of the specifics.

In 2018, I got to grips with the specifics. I learned how to find what types of properties councils are specifically looking to build more of, what their target is and how many properties they aim to see built, what the timeframes are and even which councils are falling behind on their targets. This information was pure gold!

I also found dozens of sites which had been declined planning permission and was able to study the reasons for refusal. Flooding risk is just one of many possible reasons.

As a developer it was truly liberating to become fully versed in the world of planning decisions in England and gain an understanding of why councils approve or reject planning applications. As a citizen of the United Kingdom I also found it to be extremely satisfying and enlightening.

I found I actually agree with the councils' stance on planning matters and no longer view local authorities as enemies. They are on our side and they love professional property developers. They need more houses and we are offering to build them. Councils are delighted for developers to build and make money. They just need you to not break any planning regulations which are in place for good reasons.

***

I received a Facebook message out of the blue from an investor called John who I have known for a few years. He had been investing in property for the previous ten years and wanted to move into development. He had a handful of HMOs around Birmingham and had recently had a similar situation to mine with land he was struggling with. I asked him his situation and he sent me the following reply on Messenger:

> 'It's plenty big enough, but the council won't play ball and I've now been refused planning permission twice to build. Happy now to just sell and get my money back, or will just land bank.'

The site was in a solid part of Birmingham and I knew the area really well because I had many property investments close by. I called John and had a 25-minute conversation with him. John was in a pickle and I could help him.

The reason John had been refused planning permission was because he was applying to build six apartments. There was frankly no way they would ever accept this as it was completely not in keeping with the area and there was insufficient parking for six compact apartments either. Rather than John thinking outside the box, he had lost all hope and wanted to sell the land to somebody else. Applying for planning again and again was getting expensive as well as demoralising.

From looking at the site on Google Earth I could instantly see that there was plenty of room to build two decent sized semi-detached houses about 80 square meters each. I knew within minutes that this would have an extremely high chance of being accepted because the entire street was filled with similar houses and the land was an infill with similar properties on either side of it. It was just begging to have a pair of semis built on it!

I only knew this because I had immersed myself in the world of planning and had gained a deep understanding of the criteria local authorities use to make decisions. They needed more semi-detached houses but they did not have a shortage of flats. Also, flats would clearly look out of place because there were no other flats in sight. I could see there was no flood risk and the land did not look contaminated in any way.

John was embarrassed about the situation and I felt sorry for him, having been there myself. The fact that he had said land banking was an option told me he did not need the money straight away. He just wanted an exit door and felt out of his depth. Unlike Kevin, I did not charge him £10,000 for bogus advice and neither did I offer to joint venture with him. I offered to help him with it for free, just to get him out of the situation.

Unfortunately, John was completely done with the site and had vowed never to apply for planning permission again.

He had wasted too much time on it and now just wanted the council to turn up at his door with a bunch of flowers and an apology letter, agreeing to let him build his ugly, random looking block of flats. This of course was never going to happen.

"You bought the land for £200,000," I said, "Do you regret it?"

"Well, I do now," he replied.

"How about I give you £200,000, but in 12 months, once I've had time to use my expertise to acquire the appropriate drawings and planning permission. How does that sound?"

"But what if you can't get planning permission?"

I hit him with logic:

"Then you have lost nothing. I'll pay for the drawings and the planning applications, as well as our legal agreement. If I can't get planning, I'll hand it you back and it is no different from you land banking it. If I do get planning, you get your £200,000 back."

After speaking to his wife and a few weeks' worth of negotiating back and forth, he finally agreed to give me the site on an assignable purchase lease option agreement. As part of the deal, he wanted £250,000 not £200,000 if I got planning permission and exercised my right to proceed.

If my plans failed, I would simply walk away and hand it

back to him. During the weeks of negotiation I had already spoken at length to a planning consultant who agreed that I would definitely get planning for two semi-detached houses. Despite this, I was not emotional or even particularly excited, because by this point I had about 15 other similar sites I was also negotiating on. I had learned so much over the past six months.

The contract was drawn up and signed by us both. John could not sell the site to another party for at least 12 months, while I could either buy the land or assign it to someone else for the same amount at any time during the 12-month period. This is called an Assignable Purchase Lease Option Agreement and is something most property solicitors are very comfortable with. I have been involved in dozens of similar agreements in my twelve years' experience in property, but this was the first time I had done one on land.

John was really hopeful that I would succeed and get planning permission because he desperately wanted his £250,000. I love it when business is a win/win situation with everybody pulling in the same direction. John wanted no involvement but asked me to keep him posted with any news.

Within 12 weeks I was granted planning permission to build two semi-detached houses, as predicted. The Gross Development Value of the entire site once the houses were constructed was £770,000 (£385,000) per house. This was confirmed by a professional valuer and was clear from reviewing other new build houses nearby and calculating the cost per square foot. The cost to build would probably be around £100,000 each, including all professional fees.

I was so happy with this news and John was now regretting not applying for planning himself for houses instead of flats. I did not feel bad about that, though, because I had spent so long reading countless pages of SHELAA. I had also advised him to keep it, but he felt out of his depth.

I decided not to keep the land. I did not want to buy it nor did I want to build on it. I did not feel I had the experience, and I did not want to learn from my mistakes as I would rather educate myself first. However, I did sell the assignable option on to a developer for £360,000. This made me a cool £100,000 clean profit for a site that I never owned, without lifting a single shovel and with minimal risk.

Assignable Lease Options became a strategy that I really fell in love with. I carried out two more lease options that same year. One made £101,989 and the other made £99,641.

CHAPTER 8 - Building Houses Just Makes Sense

At this stage in our lives Amanda, was a relatively new mum to our one-year old, Ruby, who was born three weeks before my famous business meeting with Lord Sugar. We wanted to have more children and Amanda was overseeing our entire property portfolio while I was working on the bigger deals.

Amanda is a quantity surveyor by profession and loved the idea of getting more involved with the development business. She had fallen out of love with overseeing our property managers and wanted to off-load some of our smaller deals to invest into development deals. She always used to tell me:

> "Managing property managers can be just as demanding as managing tenants."

Amanda is very smart and she was absolutely right. Small houses had served us well and given us a great income stream and lifestyle, but to become billionaires we needed to focus purely on bigger development deals. Amanda has plenty of experience in costing up large construction projects for the likes of Coca-Cola and had also helped manage the developments of huge new-build estates. She knew only too well how much money could be made from property developments.

Shortly afterwards we were planning our next big trip to Uganda and were in conversations with the Ugandan government about building a school. Amanda said something which turned out to be game-changing for me:

> "I definitely think we can build a school in Uganda,

but I really think we need to start building on these sites in the UK too."

In that moment I realised I had been leaving money on the table by not developing the sites I was finding. I was doing the hard work of finding the sites and negotiating with the seller, but then I was handing them on a plate to developers.

I looked at some of the land I had sold on to developers, and began to run further calculations of my own. I worked out that one of the sites which had made me £100,000 had proved even more profitable for the developers who had banked twice that amount. If I had just carried out the work myself, I would have been making £300,000 plus and these were relatively small sites.

I made a decision there and then to take on the development side too. Amanda was very talented at cost management and I was very good at finding deals. Together we were a force to be reckoned with!

Instead of playing small, I was going to play big, but I was also going to ensure I had the right people in place to not only guide me, but also to share the load with me.

We started selling some of the properties we had recently acquired. We had bought them with cashflow and long-term capital gain in mind, but they no longer fitted our strategy. We sold a few for around the price we paid which was a little disappointing, but we made a huge profit on some others. All in all, we became cash rich and were ready for some new juicy developments.

If you had told me a few years earlier that I would be

selling properties, I would not have believed it. My plan was always to accumulate and never sell. We have still got a large property portfolio of buy-to-lets, but shrinking the portfolio was actually a really good feeling.

Having a large social media following makes you acutely aware of how closely people watch and judge you. I have been abused online for 'stealing properties from the poor' and 'monopolising people's homes.' Certain individuals even hold me responsible for the housing crisis and pricing first time buyers out of the market! You could not make it up!

There is, of course, room for everyone in the property market. Providing affordable homes, albeit in shared housing, is a hugely valuable service for many sectors of society, which is appreciated by councils, landlords and tenants alike.

When you are known for making money people will always be unhappy and find fault. It is so rewarding to be doing exactly the opposite of what people have accused me of doing for many years.

My new plan was to buy land and build houses. This was helping with the housing shortage and providing good homes for people where previously there were none.

In 2018, I became obsessed with the idea of building new homes and restoring old run down buildings. I later went on to buy a castle, Ribbesford House which I will soon tell you about.

CHAPTER 9 - Why I Lent Millions To Others

During the summer of 2018, Amanda fell pregnant again with our second child. This was just after we had purchased the castle and had a lot of new sites in the pipeline.

Amanda suggested I speak to her brother, Ben, a chartered surveyor, to see whether I could persuade him to join the team as we were about to have a lot of sites on our plate.

I did not want to put Amanda under too much pressure. I also knew that without a solid business foundation and team structure in place, we could end up growing too quickly.

Property development is probably the most lucrative business on the planet, but you would be naive to think you cannot lose a lot of money if you drop the ball. I spoke to Ben and found he was very open to the idea of working together, but he was in the middle of some major developments and did not want to let his team down.

I could have looked for another person to take on the role, but I was really set on Ben. He is extremely smart and I knew he and I would make an incredible addition to the team. He was also very well connected and had a good character.

The fact that he refused to leave his current team despite me offering him eye watering amounts of money, showed he was a loyal team player. That is a trait I greatly value.

I decided that the smartest way to operate for the next 12

months would be to joint venture with other developers who were happy to take responsibility for project management while we waited for Ben to finish his projects in Leeds.

I put out some feelers to contacts that I deemed trustworthy and told them my plans. Within a matter of days my inbox was flooded with development opportunities that needed funding. I had millions to invest and was going to be funding other people's deals, while at the same time building my own network, experience, knowledge and team.

This is a smart way to start out in property development because you are getting paid from the profits, but do not have the sole responsibility of ensuring projects go smoothly. It was surprisingly hard to find good projects to fund and I had plenty of people pitching completely awful deals. I have documented some of them on YouTube, but many of these so-called 'developers' insisted on confidentiality, probably because they would have been exposed for being absolute amateurs!

I came across an 'experienced' developer who was moving on to bigger deals. He had unearthed a piece of land in Wolverhampton, a place I know very well. It was a brownfield site that had previously been used by car sales garages. Full planning permission had been granted for the construction of four houses. This was how the potential deal fleshed out:

> Purchase price: £150,000
> Development cost: £400,000 including professional fees
> Gross Development Value: £800,000

There seemed to be a great opportunity to make a profit of about £250,000. The developer wanted me to finance the land with him arranging a bridging loan for the £400,000 development cost. We would go 50/50 on the profit.

It appeared at first to be a decent little deal, but it then transpired that the land was contaminated. In essence, the soil was toxic and not suitable for development unless it was cleaned up.

The developer was confident that it would not cost much to get rid of the bad soil, but he had not factored this into the costs. I insisted he get a contamination report on the land before we proceed.

The report came back and it was bad! We would need to remove an enormous amount of soil which could end up costing more than £100,000. This made the deal so unviable I would not have got out of my bed even if the land was being offered for free!

A good deal on paper is not necessarily a good deal in reality. I could fill an entire book with stories about developers pitching opportunities to me that came with peculiar and deal-killing problems. The list includes access problems, ransom strips and protected trees. There were many good projects that I did invest in, either as a joint venture partner or as an angel investor, but sometimes you learn more from the bad deals than the good ones.

I am going to tell you about Asif's deal in Liverpool next because it is a truly X-rated horror story that will leave your jaw resting somewhere near your feet!

CHAPTER 10 - Avoiding The Classic Development Scam

Asif, a young developer from London, was close to completing on a £300,000 piece of land in Liverpool. The site had full planning permission to build five large detached houses that would each be worth an estimated £380,000.

The landowner who had bought the site was also a developer. He had built one property already and easily sold it for £380,000. He was going to use the money to build the next house and do the same until he had finished all six houses. Planning permission was granted for all the houses and everything was ready to go.

The story went that the seller had tragically lost his wife and subsequently all interest in developing the site. He was a grieving widower with no inclination to continue. He was selling the remainder of the plot for a knock-down price of £300,000 with scope to build another five high value houses.

I agreed to meet Asif in person to go over the numbers. Asif presented the figures to me from an impressive, professional looking folder. This is how the deal appeared to stack up:

> Purchase price: £300,000
> Development cost: £700,000 including contingencies.
> Professional fees and CIL: £150,000
> Gross Development Value: £1,900,000

CIL is the Community Infrastructure Levy. It is the levy

paid to the local authority as a contribution towards infrastructure costs. This has largely replaced SECTION 106 which is a similar tax in most areas across the UK and is something that must be considered before taking on any development project.

With a total end value of £1.9m, there seemed to be enough cushion in the deal for any small unknowns. I was very interested in this opportunity and I really liked Asif. He spoke well, had builders in place to start construction and was completely ready to go.

In addition, he had put together some fine spreadsheets which included full drawings, costings, market comparables and sure enough there was proof of full planning permission being granted for all five luxury houses.

His proposal was flawless. He was asking that I fund the entire site and he would give me 40% of the profits. The seller wanted a quick sale so Asif was suggesting that I put in the £300,000 cash and then we would try to get development finance for as much of the build cost as possible.

He wanted to set up a company together whereby I put down £300,000 and he would take care of everything else. I might need to put in more money further down the line for the build, but we would be on track to make £750,000. I would get all my money back plus about £300,000. Asif was confident we would get development finance and I would double my money.

It seemed like a no-brainer as everything stacked up on paper. All the professionals were signing it off as a perfect development opportunity. I asked my brother-in-law Ben's opinion, and he confirmed that Asif was spot on with the build cost. However, something did not feel quite right.

> "How confident are you on the saleability of the end product?" I asked Asif

> "Samuel, the seller just sold one of the new builds for £380,000 and it didn't even make it to the open market," he replied. "Liverpool is booming right now. Our houses will be identical to the one that just sold for £380,000. The estate will be worth at least £1.9m and maybe more by the time it is finished as prices are rising."

I know Liverpool pretty well, and £380,000 sounded very high to me. I asked Asif if he had spoken to other agents about the area.

> "It is an up-market part of Liverpool and the houses are large five-bed luxury houses," he replied.

I opened up my laptop and began searching for houses being sold nearby. In the same street there were four bedroom houses selling for £100,000. I showed Asif and he began to argue with me.

> "Samuel, you cannot compare 15-year-old houses with these new-builds. And besides they're smaller."

I found some new-builds less than 0.5 miles away which had sold two years earlier for £115,000. Asif insisted they were much smaller and remained adamant that our houses would be worth £380,000 once finished.

I found the exact square footage for the other new-builds from EPC certificates which are freely available online when you know where to look. I calculated the exact value of our five-bed detached properties using the like-for-like measurements. They would each be worth just £175,000 once finished!!!

Asif was shocked and embarrassed. He insisted we call more agents and get some independent opinions. Every agent we spoke to confirmed that we would not get a penny more than £200,000.

> "But how on earth did the seller get £380,000 for the first property then?!"

I had a look on the Land Registry and could not believe my eyes. The seller had sold the house to….. himself! Holy Moly!

The amount of times I have heard the same classic story from sellers saying their wife had died and they have now lost interest in a development. Call me cynical, but I always watch out for these types of tricks. Asif was furious with the seller and was horrified that he came so close to being scammed. I told Asif not to be annoyed with the seller, but to be mad with himself for not carrying out his proper research before trying to get me to put my cash into the site!

CHAPTER 11 - Why I Bought A Castle?

The best way to learn about property development is to do it yourself. At this particular point of my venture into the world of development, I had invested millions of pounds into other people's projects as a silent partner or 'angel investor.' As a result I only had £400,000 left in the bank. I was now ready to take on a deal of my own with the remaining money I had. Having been born and raised in The Midlands, England, I wanted to find a large building that was in need of restoration, local to my home patch.

My brother, Russell, is an extremely sharp cookie and ridiculously competitive. He had initially built up his wealth through various other kinds of business but was now also investing heavily in real estate.

Russell owned several successful companies including a lettings agency in Wolverhampton. He had systemised them well and was now was looking for his next venture. I told him to sell all his companies and come to work with me instead. I offered to make him Managing Director of my training and development company. He politely declined the invitation.

I knew Russell was going to end up selling his companies and I predicted he would use the money to scale up his own property developments. I did not want this to happen. Russell was not the kind of person you wanted to have as a competitor. He would not sleep until he was at the top of the tree. The last thing I wanted was to have him competing against me.

I arranged a business lunch with him at Lichfield Golf Club and explained to him how my development company was ready to explode. I showed him all the deals I was invested in. I sold him on my vision to have the world's leading real estate education company and wanted him to be part of it. Russell was well aware of my successes and vision, and suggested I should make him an offer.

I came up with £350,000 as a basic annual salary, with bonuses on top. He laughed and responded:

"I could make that on a single property deal, but I'm happy to partner with you on a 50/50 basis."

We spent weeks negotiating before coming to an agreement. It was a complex deal and we both appointed our own solicitors and valuers. The end result was that he sold his companies and bought into mine. We became partners with an equal share of the business.

I eventually alighted on a property to buy with my remaining £400,000 – a large commercial office block in Wolverhampton. The building was beautiful and fully occupied with commercial leases all in place. The price was £950,000 and the returns were around 15%. It was a solid investment as you have no responsibility for maintenance with commercial deals. Getting a mortgage would also be a breeze and the value would likely appreciate over time.

Despite all this, my gut was telling me not to buy. It all stacked up on paper and there were no red flags, but my inner voice was still yelling 'no.' I am famous for preaching 'formulas over feelings', but there is a big difference between feelings and intuition. Feelings are often based on preferences or irrational fears, but intuition and gut instincts are bed fellows you do not want to mess with.

There was a live auction taking place near Birmingham that I really wanted to attend. On offer was a '20-bedroom castle' that was being hyped in the newspapers. It immediately caught my attention and imagination.

Russell went to view it and showed me the video footage he had taken. We talked in depth about the possibility of restoring it. Unfortunately, I was on holiday celebrating my birthday on the day of the auction, but Russell agreed to go.

The building was set in eight acres of land in a sought-after part of Worcestershire in the Midlands. Despite being called Ribbesford House, it was actually a castle. I guess it is similar to the Queen's 'Sandringham House' also being a castle. I just love how quaint and understated aspects of British life can be!

It is imperative to carry out extensive due diligence before buying any property at auction. It is also vital that you set your maximum bid before you arrive. Auctioneers will use clever tactics to get you to bid higher than you probably should, by saying things like,

> 'You're not going to let this guy beat you, are you Sir?'

It can quickly become an ego-driven environment where emotions take over. I have coined my own saying to emphasise the dangers: 'When emotions are high, be extra careful what you buy!." Set your absolute maximum offer in concrete before you attend.

To work out what your offer should be you need to know two vital figures:

1) How much money is needed to restore/build the property?
2) What will the end value be once all works are complete?

Once you have the two answers you can work backwards.

Simply deduct 25% from the end value.

Then deduct the total money needed to restore/build the property.

The figure you are left with is your maximum purchase price.

Example:

1) £1,000,000 to restore the property
2) £3,000,000 new end value

£3,000,000 x 0.75% = £2,250,000

£2,250,000 - £1,000,000 = **£1,250,000**

So, in this hypothetical example, I would start lower but would not bid a penny higher than £1,250,000. That is because you should always aim to make a 25% profit of the Gross Development Value. This will enable you to easily secure finance on the build costs. It might be simplistic, but this is the exact formula I now use for just about every development deal I ever do. I always throw in the professional fees, CIL, finance costs and possible contingencies in my 'cost to restore' calculations.

This is all part of the due diligence process you need to carry out before thinking about bidding on a property at auction. Remember once you place a bid, you are legally obliged to buy the property for the amount you agreed to pay. That is how auctions work so tread carefully.

There was a big problem, though, with my usual due diligence process. This property was not a normal property. It was not a straightforward piece of land, or even just a big renovation. Every surveyor I spoke to refused to even attempt to put a price on the restoration. The report revealed:

1) Serious structural problems (cost unknown)
2) Riddled with Japanese Knotweed (cost unknown)
3) Roof had fallen down (est. £500,000)
4) Located on Greenbelt (issues to build on site)
5) Huge amount of dry rot and wood decay (cost to rectify unknown)
6) High chance of bats and other protected animals (could delay/prevent works)
7) Grade Two Star Building which is one step down from a Palace (everything is protected)
8) Protected Trees (PTOs) were blocking the building
9) New Configuration Needed (all dependent on planning)
10) Complete Renovation Required (cost unknown as everything is protected)

On top of this, there were so many other unknowns. The building was so protected it was not just a case of consulting the local authority to carry out any works, but also English Heritage and several other bodies. Estimating the true cost of works was near impossible. It was equally difficult to estimate the end value because the valuer would need to know the exact plans for the building, which we had already established were impossible to know.

> Generally speaking, I would never advise anybody to bid on a property such as this. It was definitely a remarkable building with an extraordinary history, but it was not for the faint hearted. However, I still felt very drawn to this building. I really wanted to restore it and had a very good intuition about it.

If I had asked any reputable professional what the better investment was between the castle and the commercial offices – I do not think any would have said the former!"

I suspect they would have all pointed to the commercial offices. But as James Caan from Dragons Den says,

> 'Observe the masses and do the opposite.'

Nobody was interested in this castle. All other developers were scared off by the multitude of unknowns. I had a lot of developments going on at the time and they were all small fry compared to this one. I knew that the potential was massive, but the problem would be getting permission to restore the castle in a way that would make it profitable. I had a few days of thinking time before the auction. Realistically, it would take many months and cost tens of thousands of pounds just to get the surveys and reports we needed.

I had become very friendly with some local planning consultants and had learned exactly how councils make decisions. Most developers hate working with English Heritage but I knew that they were desperate to see this castle restored to its former glory. The only way I was going to be able to make an informed decision on this one, was to listen to my gut and make friends with the right people. This was possible, and if anybody could pull it off, it was going to be me.

I calculated that the castle would be worth many millions once complete and the authorities would surely not prohibit the works from taking place. I told Russell to bid up to £810,000 and not a penny more.

The day of the auction Russell was outbid. We were the second highest bidder but it sold to a gentleman for £820,000. We were gutted but at least we had stuck to our guns and not got carried away with emotion. The following day I received a call from the auctioneer.

> 'Samuel, you were the second highest bidder at £810,000. We have had a problem with the buyer and would like to take your offer of £810,000. Are you still happy to proceed?'

There were many other bidders below me and I knew that if I asked for time to think about it, they would simply sell to somebody else. I had already made my decision. I agreed.

> "Wonderful, let's proceed."

I paid the £81,000 non-refundable deposit and had 30 days to pay the remaining £729,000. I only had about £300,000 in the bank now and it would be impossible to mortgage such a dilapidated building. I had £125,000 expected to come in any minute from a separate lease option agreement so I decided to apply for bridging finance of £400,000. This was all a little bit tight but in the worst-case scenario I could just pull the money from another house. I was not short of assets but getting the cash at the drop of a hat was an issue.

It is always far easier when you use a broker for any type of finance because going to the banks direct is a laborious nightmare. A broker will have access to all the different lenders and will find the best rate and the most suitable type of loan for the given purpose. They will also save you a lot of time and hassle filling out a painful amount of paperwork only to potentially see your request for finance declined. Basically always use a mortgage broker for bridging! The only broker I use these days is BenchMark Mortgages whom I now have an excellent partnership with. They have been flipping fantastic so deserve the shout out.

My usual mortgage broker at that time had always been quite slow with bridging finance and I needed the money within 30 days otherwise I could lose the castle and forfeit my £81,000 deposit. I decided to try a new broker who was known for being fast. His name was Michael and he assured me:

> 'You will have the £400,000 in time I am sure, but you will have to pay 15% interest on the loan.'

That was a lot of interest, but I was not too bothered because I didn't have the cash and even if I did, my investments were generating more than 15%. I agreed and paid Michael his small fee for brokering the deal. Ten days passed and I still had not had 100% confirmation that the loan was secured. As a result my £125,000 lease option money was delayed. I began to get nervous, especially as I had announced on social media that I was going to be the proud owner of this castle.

Two weeks went by and I was chasing the heck out of Michael. He was telling me it should be fine but to be patient. It was not about being patient, it was about ensuring I was not going to lose the deal! After 19 days, Michael called me and I just knew it was going to be bad news. I did not even let the phone ring once before answering.

"Yes, Michael?"

Michael cheerfully said,

"Hello Samuel, how are you today?"

I did not have time for small talk so I sharply responded:

"That all depends on whether this bridging money comes in. What's happening?!"

The news was not good.

"Unfortunately, due to the vast amount of work required, the Japanese knotweed and general uncertainty of the project, the lender has declined lending. We might need to look for another lender."

What the heck!? He did not even sound like he gave a monkeys. I was so angry with Michael. What an absolute prat!

"But Michael, didn't they know that from the start?' I asked as my heart was sinking into my stomach."

"I do apologise and will be happy to refund your broker fee," Michael said.

"Unless of course you want me to look for another lender?"

It was almost like this was an every day occurrence for Michael. He did not sound sorry at all, he sounded scripted.

"I don't care about the broker fee." I snapped.

"I care about losing this deal due to messing around. Please don't bother trying to find another lender, I will find another broker."

Michael sounded surprised, but remained professional and wished me the best of luck. After I calmed down I realised that Michael had not really done anything wrong. This was part of the process and he had tried his best. Why would Michael be heartbroken? Afterall it was not his castle at stake. He was just a broker trying his best.

I rang my solicitor and told him the situation. He advised me that even if I did not have the finance in time, most sellers would be patient and I should be OK. Everybody seemed relaxed except me. Of course they were, it was not their castle.

My solicitor put me in touch with another broker who was confident he could sort me out. I applied for another bridging loan of £400,000, but this time I was pessimistic about getting it in time. I could not bear hanging around for the lender to make a decision like a hungry puppy desperately waiting for its dinner.

I had the crazy idea to meet the owner and see if I could persuade him to sell me the castle on an option agreement. If not, a delayed sale would work, or even a partially delayed sale.

I did not necessarily have the money ready, but I did have my world class negotiating skills and ability to make a deal. I contacted the owner by phone and he was very open and agreed to meet me the following week. The clock was ticking, but if he was willing to meet me to discuss the matter, surely he would not force me to complete once the 30 days were up.

Securing a castle on a lease option agreement was my biggest ever challenge! I badly needed this to come off. On arrival, I was greeted with warmth and love. The owner was extremely sad to be letting the building go, but he did not have the funds to restore it and he was very old.

His knowledge of the building and its history was immense. He explained that the Free French soldiers had trained there during World War Two before two thirds of them lost their lives in the war.

Charles De Gaulle, former President of France, would regularly visit along with Winston Churchill and other well-known legendary figures. René Marbot was one of the last surviving soldiers who was based at the castle during the war. He was now aged 96 and was President of L'Association du Souvenir des Cadets de la France Libre.

I was in awe as the owner majestically took us on a tour of the building.

I presented the idea of a delayed sale to him and he said he would get back to me. I was hopeful but was not holding my breath. I told my solicitor what had happened and even he began to get a little worried.

> "I have just heard from the vendor's solicitor and you have been given forced notice to complete," he said.

> "They are not waiting and have refused your offer of a delayed sale. If you don't get the money in ten days, you will lose your £81,000 and the property."

I rang my broker and asked him for an update, he said it was possible but not likely that the money would come in on time as the lender still had not made a definite decision. There was no way I had time to refinance any of my existing properties and even if the £150,000 came in from my lease option, that would not be enough. I needed £729,000 and I only had £300,000. It was all getting seriously stressful!

If I could not get the money I would lose the deal. I would also be known as the guy who tried to buy a castle but could not afford it and lost his deposit. What would that do to my reputation?!

I could not sleep that night. I kept thinking about how badly I wanted to complete on it. It was so annoying to think that I had millions in property, but it was all tied up and I could not access it fast enough.

Amanda then suggested I should contact some my investor friends to see if they might be interested.

> "I could try," I replied, "but it's very short notice and they wouldn't have time to register charges and carry out the correct processes for money lending."

Amanda was not going to let me give up that easily!

> "Champions do not try – they choose to do, or not to do. Are you going to do whatever it takes to get the funds or are you going to pull out of the deal?"

It is so annoying when people repeat words that you usually say to others, but she was right, as always.

The following morning I started phoning high net worth investors that I had good relationships with. I explained the situation and offered a 10% return on investment. Usually it was me giving money to developers, not the other way around. Within four hours, I had the contracts signed for the full £400,000 and the next day the full amount was sitting in my bank. I could not believe how easy it was.

Literally minutes after the £400,000 hit my bank account, I received a call from my new mortgage broker:

> "Samuel, good news! The lender is happy to give you the £400,000 and is ready to send the monies."

Oh snap! I did not even need the bridging finance any more. I told my broker I did not want the money but was happy to pay his fee anyway. I apologised for wasting his time. He was very surprised and it sounded like he had never dealt with an investor as manic as me before, but he accepted. I rang Russell to tell him what happened, and he suddenly interrupted my explanation:

> "Excellent, so you did end up getting the castle on a no money down basis, well done!"
>
> "Russell", I said, "I'm confused. I didn't take the bridging finance. We don't need both lots of £400,000."
>
> "You're right, we don't NEED it," he said, "but it means we can then use our £320,000 for something else, like leverage to buy more developments."

I liked his thinking. I called the broker instantly and agreed to take both lots of money. We bought the castle the next day and did not put a penny of our own money down.

CHAPTER 12 - Lessons Learnt From The Castle, Ribbesford House

The main reason why I wanted to become a millionaire had nothing to do with money. It was about who I could become by going through the process of making it. In the same way, as much as I wanted to buy and develop a castle, the strongest reason behind it was the lessons I would learn and the developer I would become through the experience.

Doing What Needs To Be Done

A few months after completing on the castle I flew to Uganda to check the progress of some water tanks we had constructed in rural villages. I took a small group of mentees with me, all of whom had recently become successful property investors.

On the first day, our guide took us on water rafting adventure on the River Nile, as a team-building exercise which was an utter disaster. In fact I was lucky to escape with my life after the boat capsized. I was flung out of the raft as it plunged down a waterfall and suffered a very serious knee injury after being dashed against the rocks. I lost a quarter of my blood and had to have emergency surgery. I spent ten days in a local hospital with practically no food and at times spent hours lying in my own urine. The surgeon, Jamela, was incredible but the aftercare was very different to the UK. When I finally got home to England an NHS doctor told me I was lucky to be alive.

I was fortunate to have been in a position to be able pay

for the surgery, because in many developing countries you can be left to die if you have not got the means to pay.

When I got home, I was in tears at the thought of people being rushed to the same hospital in Uganda only to be refused treatment. I contacted my Ugandan surgeon and she told me how she sometimes had to resort to begging for funds in the streets so she could treat seriously injured patients. Part of the Samuel Leeds Foundation now helps to support people in this situation and Jamela and I have remained friends to this day.

On leaving Uganda I was supposed to be meeting Robert Kiyosaki for a dinner before returning to England, but had to cancel due being in hospital.

Kiyosaki is an extremely wealthy real estate investor and author of the book, Rich Dad Poor Dad, a book that had really impacted on my life ten years earlier. I was gutted to have missed the opportunity to spend an evening with him.

The following year, however, he came to London to speak at a conference. I paid £50,000 to book a beautiful private room in the same hotel where Kiyosaki kindly agreed not only to have dinner with me, but also meet twenty-five of my mentees.

We had a fabulous evening, during which I publicly interviewed him and facilitated an open Q+A session. At one point during the interview, he rudely interrupted me as I was stressing the importance of people doing what they love to do.

"How selfish," he snapped. "Stop telling people to

do what they love!"

I could not believe what I was hearing. Of course people should do what they love. I wanted to argue with Robert, but he is a 74-year-old living legend. Instead I politely asked him to explain what he meant.

"Everybody is doing what they love, but so few are doing what needs to be done," he said.

I did not really understand what he was talking about at the time, but smiled and moved on with the interview. Upon reflection later, it dawned on me that maybe I needed to focus less on myself and more on others. The only reason I was helping the hospitals in Uganda was because I had gained first-hand experience of being a patient at that same hospital. Maybe I had been there for a reason? Not as a punishment but because something needed to be done.

Returning to the subject of my castle, I was delighted to receive a letter from none other than René Marbot, one of the last remaining war heroes who had trained at Ribbesford House. René was 96-years-old and was very keen to meet me.

He organised a small party in Mayfair, London and even flew his sons in from France for the occasion. I felt honoured to be there and we were both delighted that the Anglo-French connection was going to be preserved.

René told us his memories of what had gone on inside the castle during the war. I assured him that the French plaque outside the building would remain in place and we were going to do whatever it took to restore this sentimental building. René was a true war hero and deserved to have his wishes granted. He seemed relieved and overjoyed to hear that the building would not be left to waste away.

He held my hand, looked me right in the eye and said: "Thank you for doing what needs to be done."

That was the last time I spoke to René before he died. For me, property development became not just something that made money, but something that needed to be done.

Abundance Brings More Abundance

One of the reasons I had struggled to get bridging finance on the castle, was not just because the building was a wreck, but also because I did not have a proven track record of restoring protected buildings.

I had been a successful property investor for ten years and had no issue getting finance for HMOs or Buy-to-Lets, but lenders want to see other sites you have developed before lending cash for property projects. Luckily, I had invested in some other developments and was able to provide some assurance that I knew what I was doing, but nothing similar to Ribbesford House.

Many people assume they can start developing sites and lenders will throw money at them, but if lenders are not confident of your abilities they will not back your deals. I was now putting myself on the map as a property developer and people were taking me more seriously. I was no longer just investing in other people's deals and reassigning option agreements, I was developing an historic 20,000 square ft castle set in eight acres of private woodland.

My standing as a property developer was also starting to be acknowledged by various celebrities. On one occasion I was enjoying a Mediterranean Cruise when I received a brief message from my brand manager, Amelia Asante, which made me sit up and pay attention:

> "James Caan from Dragons Den wants to talk to you."

I was taken aback that such a famous TV star wanted me to phone him but was very curious to hear the agenda. It turned out that Amelia had arranged for the two of us to make a video together for YouTube, but he wanted to have a private meeting as well.

James had long been one of my heroes in business and I had watched dozens of people on TV pitching to him for investment on Dragons Den.

I called James and he was very business-like and began firing questions at me about my business. It felt like a private version of Dragons Den and I enjoyed sharing with him exactly how my business plan worked and answering his difficult and direct questions.

James seemed very impressed with Ribbesford House and began to tell me how his business works. He said he was looking to invest in private developments such as the castle.

> "If you ever have another project that needs financing like that castle, please do send me a proposal," he said.

How did I go from struggling to get the finance for the castle, to buying it with none of my own money, to now being approached by a famous Dragons Den star who has millions of pounds?

The answer of course is that success breeds success. Success is the start of a train reaction, the start of a money avalanche. It is much easier to raise cash when you already have money yourself. Desperation is a terrible place to be in for any developer, but abundance leads to more abundance.

Being Out Of Control

Most entrepreneurs are control freaks which is why they can not work for anybody else. The problem is that when you start a business some things are out of your control. I am an optimist by nature and was hoping the development of Ribbesford House would be fast paced. I was excited about configuring the plans for the apartments and putting a full planning application forward to start the works. Unfortunately, this was not possible.

There was an overwhelming number of things to think about. Should we start by getting planning permission for the full works? Or should we first make the building safe and replace the broken roof? Should we underpin the foundations or prioritise eradicating the Japanese knotweed? All the experts were giving conflicting advice as to where we should begin.

My 'brother' Ben, the chartered surveyor, is greatly experienced at delivering sites of this nature. He has worked on numerous Grade II listed buildings as Project and Cost Manager. The most challenging was a Grade II listed school that was transformed into a thriving business incubation centre.

I felt very comfortable knowing that within a few months, Ben would be setting up a company called MacLeeds with us. It would be a joint partnership with the sole purpose of managing our development sites. Ben had some great ideas for Ribbesford, but it was not going to be a rapid process.

Before Ben came onboard, we did undertake a few safe-making and enabling works that were necessary to lay the foundation for restoration of this awesome building.

Ben's advice to me was to be patient. There was no urgency to get the building finished quickly and there was no point starting works without a plan. We paid off most of the bridging finance because it was expensive, but began focusing on building relationships with the community. We got to know local planning officers, ecologists and of course members of English Heritage.

We began by getting permission to remove many of the protected trees that were blocking the views and creating damp problems to the building. We cleared all the rubbish from the site and managed to burn all the Japanese knotweed from the grounds.

We secured up to £10m worth of insurance to prevent the risk of knotweed returning in the future. We found a spring that was shooting water underground at the foundations of the building and causing structural problems. In addition to all the repointing work, the building needed underpinning to make it structurally sound.

All this important work was adding immense value to the building, but more importantly it was also preventing the building from deteriorating. We also got high powered security systems in place and employed a full-time caretaker and gardener. His name is Simon and he lives rent free in one of the houses on the premises.

Once all this work was completed, it was time to decide how many apartments and houses we could get onto the estate. This had to be done in a tasteful way and in keeping with the grounds, history and area. At the same time it had to be worth our while as developers.

The council fully appreciated that the development had to make a profit to be viable. I was impressed with how patient I remained throughout this process. However, we now had a major problem on our hands. Bats!

There were bats in the building, and they were not just any bats. They were a rare and protected species. We had to hold off on everything, until we had had a full ecologist's report.

This would advise exactly how we were to deal with the bats and how we would re-house them. That would not be possible until the following year because we needed to ensure it was the right season for the bats to be moved. I thought tenants had a lot of rights, but it seems bats have more rights than the Queen! They were certainly driving us all bat-shit-crazy!

To make matters worse in the middle of this frustrating hold up, the entire world suddenly announced it was going into a complete lockdown due to coronavirus. Builders were running out of materials and the economy was collapsing all around us. The virus apparently originated with, you guessed it, a bat! It seemed that my world was crumbling because of blessed bats.

Ben kept things completely under control and we informed the media that the works were being paused due to the pandemic and the bats. I had to remind myself that it was not going to be any less profitable, it was just going to be a long-term project. I learned the art of true patience.

When something is completely out of your timescale and control, you just have to move on and wait patiently. I had previously been jumping up and down, pointlessly chasing and spending lots of energy trying to speed up something which I had no control over.

Rather than being frustrated with Ribbesford House, I decided to enjoy the journey and savour the process. Although I could not rent the castle to anybody in its current state, I began thinking of how I could monetise it in the meantime. I listed it as a castle ruin and allowed people to rent it for the day for filming purposes.

Within two weeks we had a call from some major movie producers who were prepared to pay handsomely. I could not believe my luck. I cannot say too much about this, but all I will say is I am excited to be watching Netflix in the coming years and when the time is right you will know which film was recorded at Ribbesford House.

When the ball is in your court, you need to knock it out. When it is not, you need to be patient and wait for it. There is no point stressing over what you cannot control.

Once the castle was made safe and the urgent issues had been dealt with, I began to hold meetings with the council about what we should do with the building. It had previously been used as 12 apartments and 4 houses, and getting planning for 12 apartments and 8 houses was pretty much a given.

However, we needed to put forward the best application that would not only do the building justice, but also make it as profitable as it needed to be to justify the works. I paid £6,000 to have an Independent chartered surveyor to value the castle based on just 12 apartments and 8 houses. Maybe sceptics had said it would only be worth a few million and it would cost that to renovate it. I was very nervous about the official Red Book Valuation.

I was delighted to read in the report that the Gross Development Valuation had been put at £6,350,000.

Shortly afterwards, Russell came over to my house and asked if I had received the figure.

It was the perfect opportunity to play a little prank on him. Bear in mind we had paid £810,000 initially and had since invested £1,000,000 on the works. There was still a lot more to do and we were £1.8m in. I would never usually do this and there is no way he would expect me to trick him. I just thought it would be funny as we had waited so long for this valuation.

> "Russell, I am stunned with the valuation. It is extremely low."
>
> "Go on?" he said.

"The Gross Development Value has come in at £2,000,000 only."

Russell fell about laughing:

"We really messed up on this one didn't we! Oh well!"

This would have not only been a financial tragedy for us with a £4,000,000 shortfall, but also personally devastating. Yet Russell had just laughed. This was not because he thought I was joking, but because he understands that there are risks that you can not control and therefore you can not get too worried about. That is, of course, so long as you invest wisely and do not overstretch yourself to the point of ruin or being unable to feed your children.

The valuation was something we could estimate, but with a unique building like Ribbesford House, we could not guarantee or have any control over what the valuer would come back with.

Once Russell had recovered from my prank, we laughed loudly together, with an unspoken satisfaction. We had done our utmost in terms of due diligence and it had all paid off handsomely.

Long-Term Thinking

Patience is a lesson all property developers need to learn. Most people want immediate gratification and are used to getting paid for the work they did the previous month. You go to work and then soon afterwards the money lands in your account. As a property developer the financial rewards are larger than in most regular professions, but pay days are never immediate.

When you are working on a project you can expect to wait at least twelve months before you are actually get paid for it, sometimes a lot longer. You should always think ahead and never wait for a project to completely finish before moving on to another site. You want multiple projects on the go at the same time, plus more in the pipeline. This is why I have been continuing to buy sites whilst the castle is ticking along in the background.

The importance of taking a long-term view cannot be overstated. Even now, well before the castle is fully renovated and all the apartments/ houses have been sold, I am already thinking about the power of land banking the remaining 6 acres of land in Worcestershire.

One of my mentees was negotiating on a piece of land in Yorkshire but did not have more than £10,000 to his name. He asked me if I could finance the entire site for a 10% fixed return until he had completed the development, but such low returns do not interest me.

The site was a large plot that could comfortably accommodate twelve houses. However, because the access road was very narrow the council had only granted a maximum of five houses. Twelve families were considered too many to be driving in and out of the narrow road.

The approximate figures ran as follows:

      Asking price for land: £280,000
      Cost to build five houses: £600,000 (inc. everything

except finance fees)
Gross Development Value: £1,000,000 (£200,000 per house)

Planning permission had been granted for the five houses but, as you should be able to see from the above figures, there was only around £120,000 profit in this site.

You may think £120,000 is not bad, but you need to factor in a few stumbling blocks. For a start, it would be near impossible to get bridging finance because lenders would want to see at least 20% profit in the deal. This one was only showing about 12% profit. You can easily calculate this by dividing the GDV by the profit e.g. £120,000 divided by £1,000,000 equals 12%.

There was no way I was going to fund this site as it was a very average opportunity that most developers would turn down. However, I used the Land Registry to find out who owned the land which had the narrow road running through it. The owner was an elderly lady who was not a property developer.

I ran everything over in my mind. The only reason we could not build more than five houses was because the road was too narrow. It would be very cheap to widen the road, we would just need to get permission to buy a slither of the owner's garden. If we were to offer her £100,000, I guarantee she would accept. Even if she did not, down the line the new owners would. You always need to think ahead.

The twelve houses would not cause any nuisance to the land owner, they may even accept £20,000. If we could get permission to do this, it would increase the GDV from

£1m to a whooping £2.4m. Then it would certainly merit my interest!

I decided to buy this deal for myself and land bank it. Land banking is where you sit on your asset and wait for the right time to develop it. This is not a get rich quick tactic, more like a 'get very wealthy over an unknown period of time.'

This was my new way of thinking, and I would not have had his mind-set without the long-term strategy I had developed working with Ben on Ribbesford House. The richer I get, the luckier people will say I am, but in reality it is more down to me learning to take a long term view.

Comfort Zone Kills

If a flower is not growing, it is dying. If you are not growing you are also dying. What do I mean by growing? By growing I simply mean getting better, learning and being stretched. It is impossible to grow without being outside your comfort zone. Stepping outside your comfort zone will stretch you and put you in an environment where you are forced to get bigger.

The human mind has a job to see you safe and protect you. Its job is not to grow and thrive, but to keep comfortable and survive. Because of this, you will always have a little voice telling you all the reasons why you should not try new things, take risks or push new boundaries.

Buying the castle hurled me outside my comfort zone. It changed my perspective on what a big deal looked like, because subsequently I had become bigger myself. This has been one of the most precious lessons from Ribbesford House.

I remember taking on a site in Lincoln in 2019 to build six new houses. Everybody was talking about it online and predicting the hardships we would face. It turned out that after I had paid £330,000 to buy the land, the soil was unsuitable for the standard traditional foundation type. Usually, this problem would have been stressful. However, everything felt tiny in comparison to Ribbesford House. I was totally unfazed and knew there would be a simple solution. The solution was foundation piling, which is where you hammer steel tubes into the ground and pour concrete into the tubes. It secures the foundation and ensures the houses will not subside. This ended up costing £28,000, but hardly dented the end profit once the houses were completed in 2020.

You will always have problems in business, but the bigger you become the smaller they seem to be. Most teenagers lose sleep over their exam results, most adults stress about their wedding day. To be a billionaire you have to be very different. You better get used to dealing with huge problems and taking it in your stride. The castle really did teach me to get comfortable with being uncomfortable, and never to stay inside my comfort zone.

Ignore The Naysayers

If you are professional footballer, it must be strange having so many overweight loud mouths screaming at you and telling you how to play. They probably could not run more than fifty yards without suffering a heart attack.

It is a bit similar when you are a high profile property

developer. Every man and his dog have an opinion on what you could be doing better, or why your development will miserably fail. You have to completely ignore these backseat developers who sometimes claim to be experts.

Before taking an opinion from anybody you need to ask yourself: what have they done themselves and what is their agenda for commenting on your deals?

When we bought the land in Lincoln, I posted a YouTube video outlining our plans. I sort of regretted it afterwards because it attracted so much negativity from the 'expert' trolls.

They all said that I would not be able to build six houses for £500,000. No way! In fact, many of the people saying this were supposedly builders and experienced developers. They were wrong and we made just shy of half a million pounds profit.

The same idiots who said this deal would be a spectacular flop, then began to pour scorn over my next project, a house flip in Birmingham from which we anticipated a six-figure profit.

'It will never value up!' they mocked.

The funny thing is that the house flip was a deal where my return was 100% fixed as my role was as an angel investor not a joint venture partner. This means even if it did not value up, I would still get my share from the developers' other projects. It did value up though and they were left red-faced again.

Guess what? These were the same losers who said

Ribbesford House was a money pit. Damn right it is a money pit. I am going to collect seven-figures from my money pit!

Fortunately for me, many of my earlier deals were not published on YouTube as many developers can be very secretive. Back in 2017 it would have psyched me out seeing so much negativity from people claiming to be professionals. The only flip side would have been them saving me from that disastrous deal in Derby.

My advice now is to broadcast the heck out of your deals, and have fun proving everybody wrong when you win big. The key of course is making sure you do win big!

Ben strongly disagrees with me on this and will not allow me to publicise any deals I am doing with him, because many sellers end up giving us more and more sites. His worry is that other developers will see what we are doing and go direct to the seller to undercut us.

Ultimately, there are pros and cons of publicly documenting your developments, but I would always err on the side of doing it when appropriate if all parties agree.

Too many people talk a big game. I prefer to do the deals, make the money and let my bank account speak for itself.

CHAPTER 13 - How To Minimise Tax

Over the years, I've noticed a clear and direct correlation between the success of my mentors and my own success.

Every time I immersed myself in a new training programme, or received mentoring from somebody more successful than me, I saw a rapid spike in my business growth. I had been very impressed with Grant Cardone after meeting him for a YouTube interview at his private manor house in the outskirts of London.

At first I thought he was just a very famous motivational speaker, but after getting to know him a little bit, I discovered I was wrong. Grant owned a billion-dollar real estate company and knew far more about development than I did. He was extremely well connected and had been buying property for decades. After the YouTube interview, all he wanted to talk about was real estate. He was also very humble and sweet, very different to how he appears in many of his videos.

I felt like I could learn a lot from Cardone. Like me he can be brash and to the point, but his real estate knowledge runs very deep and his way of thinking is unique. My attitude has always been to find people more successful than me and pay them to mentor me. I now wanted Cardone as my mentor.

I flew to Miami to attend a business conference he was speaking at which cost me around £7,000. While I was there, I asked his team to arrange another meeting with me.

"You can't just meet Cardone, you have to pay," was the blunt response.

Previously I had not paid him anything, but maybe I had been lucky under the circumstances. I asked how much would it cost to have him spend some one-on-one time with me.

"That would be two hundred grand."

They gave me a contract to sign immediately. I was in two minds whether to pay the money as it could be pumped into another juicy development project. I quickly ran over the pros and cons in my mind.

Pros: If I could learn exactly how Grant had built his billion-dollar real estate company, I could do the same and get super rich. If I put the money into one property deal, it would not make me a billionaire. If I put it into my education and knowledge, the sky could be the limit. After all, it was only knowledge that got me here in the first place. If you wiped my net worth to zero I would make it back again, but if you wiped my knowledge of property to zero I would be screwed. Property is the second best investment, the best is yourself.

Cons: I might not learn anything new and it could be a waste of money. He might turn out to be a jerk and I could end up hating the mentoring sessions.

Conclusion: I figured that the potential rewards outweighed the potential risks. I signed the contract and had my first session with Grant the same week.

"This better be good," I thought as I made my way to the first meeting.

Grant trawled through my business plan in great detail. We spoke briefly about sales, marketing, investment, structure and different types of deals, but the thing we spoke about the most was finances.

He wanted to know every little detail of each company's turnover, direct costs, overheads, net profit percentage and annual targets. I wasn't prepared for that at all and probably came across as clueless at times.

I have always had in-house accountants to deal with all that while I just focused on making the money. It took a long time before I could get the correct figures for Grant and I was looking at them feeling very happy. I was making millions and I was not even thirty years old yet.

Grant stunned me when he said:

> "You are making far too much profit."

I thought I must have misheard. Surely he meant to say, I was making far too little profit. After all, he was much richer than me. He went on,

> "You're not spending enough money. Your net profit is too high and you're now being blasted with tax. Next year you'll pay seven figures in tax."

"I'm happy to pay millions in tax, if I'm making tens of millions myself," I reasoned.

"How can it be possible to make too much profit? The

purpose of a business is to make profit!"

Grant walked me through how he ran his finances and it absolutely blew me away. He was putting every penny back into not just real estate, but tax-deductible expenditure that was accelerating his business to the point where his company was worth more than a billion. He did not care about profit. To make lots of profit means you will be taxed at 50%, and then only have the remaining balance to buy stuff. Grant was just buying stuff through the business and paying less tax.

He had just bought a private jet because his state allowed him to claim most of it back as a business expense. He was legitimately putting so much stuff through the business that he did not need to be making a profit on paper.

Grant connected me to some seriously big real estate players in London and I studied how they did things. They were all spending a fortune on marketing, staff, commissions, offices, travel, accommodation and world class consultants. They were throwing all their profits back into the business, both bricks and mortar and service.

The following week I met with my newly recommended tax advisors in London. They were very expensive, but that is the point. It is a tax-deductible service. Pay for the best, be the best and pay less tax. I had previously never minded paying taxes, but Cardone was right, I needed to change the way I was doing my finances. I'll never forget his wise words:

> "You are being so frugal and conservative. You need to let money flow through you, not to you.

Bored money disappears, you have to use money or else you'll lose money."

I made a list of things that were tax deductible that would grow my business, and became extravagant with those things. I was able to write them all off as expenses and ultimately pay less tax.

This was against everything I had previously done. I was always told 'turnover is vanity, profit is sanity,' and when I told people Cardone's advice, most thought it was reckless and incorrect. However, the people saying that were nowhere near as wealthy as he was, nor did they seem to be as happy.

It is undeniable that most rich people pay very little tax. Kiyosaki argues that not paying tax is ethical because the only way to avoid taxes is to follow what the government actually wants you to do. That is why you should not pay tax.

If one of the ways you are avoiding taxes is to spend all your profits on growing your business, then you are actually pumping money back into the economy. You are being a reservoir rather than a pond.

Over the following few months, I studied tax and finance like never before. I found many ways to legally and ethically avoid paying tax. One way was to put all my giving through a registered charity, so it was tax deductible.

I had previously given much of my profits straight to building wells and to hospitals etc., but not through a charity. This was a big mistake so I finally got around to officially registering the Samuel Leeds Foundation.

One of the issues we still had, though, was we wanted to invest large amounts of our profits straight back into buying and developing land. Many types of properties are very difficult to claim back as tax deductible expenses.

We acted on many things Grant had advised us to do and watched our business boom. We rented a large central London office and had dozens of highly paid staff across the companies.

We were getting uncomfortable, but that was exactly what was needed to enable us to grow. Sadly, the global lockdown meant we had to close down the offices in London, but despite the recession our property business was going from strength to strength and we were finding more sites than we could fund. Ben was overseeing our existing projects including the castle whilst large chunks of money were flowing in from property which was being reinvested in new projects.

I started paying much more attention to my finances rather than just focusing on finding good deals, and became a mad student of figuring out new ways to reduce tax.

CHAPTER 14 - If You're So Rich, Why Borrow Other People's Money?

I had always wondered why developers bothered using other people's money. I could see why you might need to do so for your first deal. However, once you have made your profit, why would you not simply reinvest it into your next deal? Why use somebody else's money when you have your own?

Now do not get me wrong, I understand why you would use a bridging loan or a mortgage, because if you bought everything entirely in cash it would tie up too much money and would mean you could only do one site at a time. But why repeatedly borrow other people's money again and again if you are an established developer?

I was heading in the opposite direction at the time and had been putting my money into other people's deals. Now it was making less sense to do that, because my own deals were better than other people's deals.

If it was my deal, I did not have to give anybody a share. I was now fully set up with an incredible power team and had the experience to get bridging finance much more easily. I was getting so good at finding deals I could only take on two or three at a time, but that suited me.

I had another mentoring session with Grant Cardone and to be honest, I did not really have any questions for him at all that day. I was making good money and I had a good set up. I did not understand why Grant was one of those investors continually using other people's money.

The moment the consultation began he started telling me about one of his large apartment blocks. He was raising money for it and he even suggested I invest in it myself.

> "The deal looks solid," I responded, "but I have my own deals and use my own money. In fact, why do you even need my money when you are worth hundreds of millions? It doesn't make sense to me."

Grant explained that using other people's money means that he can get an infinite return on investment and he can have an unlimited amount of property. He emphasised that it is how he has grown a billion-dollar real estate portfolio.

> "I guess it does logically make sense if you want to be as rich as possible," I countered.

> "I don't just want to be as rich as possible," said Grant "I also want to help as many people as possible. Money makes things happen and I want people to remember me long after I am gone. Nobody will remember me for making a bunch of dollars, but they will remember that I helped a bunch of people."

I could not argue with Grant's points. They were logical and it made commercial sense. But it just seemed a lot of work bringing lots of other people into your deals, when you are making enough money to already do whatever you want. I put this point to Grant:

> "Thanks for explaining why you use other people's money when you have your own. For me, I'm happy doing what I am doing. I'm making good

money already and don't have the same inclination to times what I'm doing by ten."

Grant Smiled and said,

> "Oh I see, you're over the hill then. You're in your twenties and you are happy as you are. I am in my sixties and I am more hungry for success."

Grant's response really rankled me. How dare he call me 'over the hill.'

I later pondered on what he had said and realised he was right. I did not need other people's money to do a few sites at a time, but life is short and to win this game and be the biggest, I had to leverage other people's money as well as my own.

Soon after our meeting I had an offer accepted on a beautiful site that Ben had found in Leeds. It was a piece of land that had lapsed planning permission to build an apartment block consisting of five two-bed apartments. The figures were as follows:

> Purchase price: £210,000
> Development cost: £450,000
> Gross Development Value: £1,000,000
> Profit: £340,000

Let us now look at the two ways this deal would typically be financed:

Option 1: I use my own hard cash for the entire site and put down £660,000. Once the site is built and sold, I get my £660,000 back plus a profit of £340,000, meaning in total I receive £1,000,000. If all goes to plan, I will get a 51.5% return on my money, which is pretty good.

Option 2: I use my own cash to buy the land for £210,000, but then use development finance to fund the £450,000 build and give them £50,000 in interest. Once the site is built and sold, I pay the lender £500,000, get my £210,000 back plus a profit of £290,000. While my profit is a little less, I personally put down much less money. My return on money would actually be 138% which is extremely good.

You can see that option 2 is much smarter and you would have to be financially incompetent to choose option 1. Why tie money up when you can do more sites and make a significantly better return on investment?

My good friend Tony was always asking if he could invest some money into my deals. He was a millionaire but did not have much experience in property development. I had previously learnt a lot from partnering with others and Tony wanted to do the same with me. Obviously, he wanted to make some good money at the same time. He knew that buying small deals was not the way to go anymore, and he wanted to scale up but lacked the know-how. I told Tony I did not want his money and he could just watch me. He really wanted to make some money together and ended up investing with some of my students, who were also quickly becoming successful in property development from having attended my training programs.

Tony said he had invested a few hundred thousand with my students, but still had plenty of money and was really nagging me to let him in on a development deal. He offered to pay the full £210,000 for a project in Leeds, in exchange for 50% of the profit.

I did not want him to take half the profit, for doing none of the work, when I had found the deal with Ben – especially when I had had the money to invest myself.

I mentioned this to Grant Cardone who told me, in no uncertain terms, that I was mad to refuse Tony's money. Maybe I was thinking too small. Maybe I was being selfish. I decided to crunch the numbers and see what made commercial sense.

Option 3: I use Tony's £210,000 to buy the land, then use development finance to finance the £450,000 build and give them £50,000 in interest. Once the site was built and sold, I would pay the lender their £500,000, return Tony's investment of £210,000, plus have a profit of £290,000 to split between us, giving us £145,000 each. Tony would make a return on investment of 69% which is amazing, and I would make an infinite return on investment.

I decided that although I was losing £145,000 by letting Tony in on the deal, I was also saving on having to put down £210,000. It seemed reasonable all round.

Once Tony and I completed on the site, something extraordinary happened! First, Tony was overjoyed and it was extremely satisfying being able to bring somebody else into the deal. Afterall, that is what others had done for me and it is how I got started in property. But also, something else happened. Because I still had my £210,000 ready to invest, I started looking for another site. And I found somewhere. It was a very similar deal also in Leeds. I needed £185,000 to buy the land.

I had a crazy idea, what if I use another joint venture partner on this next deal? That way, I will make the £145,000 I felt Tony had taken from me, but I would not have to use any money myself.

Holy Moly! I could keep doing this again and again and just keep my £210,000 as leverage! I finally realised that Cardone was right as usual. I was so glad that I paid him that £200,000 payment for his mentorship. By the way you just got the same lesson for price of this book!

My mindset and my strategy have completely changed. Now you know exactly why rich people are happy to use other people's money!

CHAPTER 15 - My Property Development Business Plan

Most successful property developers hide away and do not share their business plans. The information found online is mostly from university students who are studying real estate but have not made a penny in this game, let alone a million.

I have made many millions of pounds doing exactly what you will learn in this chapter. My only agenda is to see you succeed and to be remembered in your success story. I hope to meet you at Property Development Secrets Live which is a live training programme that gives me the opportunity to meet my students in person and take things to the next level. Follow these final steps by the letter and you will be shocked at your results.

Finding Sellers

I am potentially going to create a lot of competition for myself by revealing these secrets in this chapter. All I ask in return is that when you get your first deal, please find me on social media and tell me.

Also, when you become a property millionaire, please remember where you learned the information and give generously to charity. It is amazing how many people forget where their learning came from once they become successful. Ok, here goes . . .

I send out a minimum of twenty-five letters per week to landowners. I use a special piece of computer software to scour potential sites using a bird's eye view of my chosen area and the software reveals who owns the land concerned. I will share all the exact software to use when I see you at Property Development Secrets Live.

The purpose of the letter is to arrange a conversation. That is all. I always include my phone number and email and ask them to get in touch should they be open to a conversation about a potential sale.

I do not make any formal offers or spend too long doing due diligence on the site. Only about 10% of owners will even acknowledge your letter, hence the reason why I send so many each week.

Appraising Sites

When potential sellers get in touch, my job is to become a detective and find out as much information as I can about the opportunity. They usually have not got a clue how much their land is worth and want me to make them an offer. The things I need to establish are:

1) What is my vision for the site? For example, what would seem suitable and profitable to build there?
2) Would it be likely to gain planning permission?
3) How much would it cost to develop?
4) Are they any red flags, such as issues with greenbelt land, high risk flooding, contamination, ransom strips etc.?
5) What is the seller's situation? I always tailor my offer to suit their needs

Skilfully appraising sites is something that comes with time and experience and I hope to have the opportunity to train you to become a master over time.

Making the Offer

Once I have appraised the site, I will usually suggest that the seller should keep the land and develop it themselves. They usually refuse this option because they do not have the skills to do so, but this is a great way to demonstrate you are not trying to take advantage of them.

I love it if they have previously applied for planning permission and failed because usually they just did it wrong. Educated developers can check out why an application was rejected and use that information to decide if a different approach is likely to prove successful.

I will then offer them the following options:

1) A Straight Cash Offer

This is, of course, subject to a survey and further due diligence. I would only do this if planning permission was already in place or if I was extremely confident that permission would be granted. I would make an embarrassingly low offer based on the land being worth the same as piece of expensive carpet.

2) A Lease Option Agreement

This is most typical option in cases where planning permission has not yet been granted. We fix a fair price, but down the line in order to give me the chance of obtaining planning permission. If planning permission is denied, I walk away but cough up the costs associated with going through the procedure. If planning permission is accepted, I make sure I win big. Sometimes you need to give them a small non-refundable deposit to sweeten the deal. Only give a deposit you can afford to lose it, should planning permission be denied.

3) A Joint Venture With The Seller

The seller probably does not need the money because you found them off-market. The seller wants as much money as they can get but does not often have the skills to develop it themselves. This is an extremely attractive offer to the seller and I usually keep this up my sleeve if they are not interested in either of the above options. An example of this would be that the seller gets their money right at the very end once the site has been developed and sold, but you take 50% of the profit from the uplift. The building cost could be funded by you, shared or it could be development finance if the land is unencumbered.

Getting the Finance

If the seller goes for anything other than Option 3, you are going to need to find the money to buy the site. It is possible to get a bridging loan for this. However, it will then be much harder to get development finance to build as the lender will want a first charge on the site. It is much easier to get finance when you have a site that is unencumbered, meaning that there is no current debt/charges registered against it.

With this in mind, I rarely get a loan to buy a site in the first place. Instead, I will find a joint venture partner, such as Tony. They will fund the purchase, while I will use my skills and experience to get development finance for the building costs.

I will then use my power team to carry out the build start to finish, and then at the end, they will get their money back plus half of the profits. This is wonderful for them, but also means I can do this many times without tying up too much cash.

If the seller goes for a lease option, even better. I will then take control of the property and then find a joint venture partner for the site.

If, for whatever reason, I do not want to take the site on or it is unsuitable, I will package and sell the opportunity to another developer. I usually receive a finder's fee of between £10,000 - £25,000 depending on the size and profitability of the deal.

Structuring the Joint Venture

A joint venture agreement can be drawn up in many ways, depending on the partner coming on board. Here are the some standard options.

1) The site goes in the name of your joint venture partner

This might sound strange, but I have seen this many times. It does not matter whose name the site is held in if you have the right contracts. What does matter is the share of profits.

I have been involved in numerous deals with wealthy music artists, footballers and other celebrities. For some reason, famous people tend to be obsessed about having everything put in their name. They are often reluctant to proceed if this is not the case. To me it is completely illogical, but it makes little odds.

I had a situation with a footballer where he agreed for me to take 80% of the profit but insisted it should be 'his' deal. Fine by me! I simply had a charge on the property and we had an airtight joint venture agreement which showed up nicely on the title deeds. I did not own the deeds, but my name was all over them in the clauses.

2) The site goes in your name.

Some partners might not want it in their name for tax or privacy reasons. You can have the site in your name and let your partner have a joint venture agreement as described above.

3) Set up a joint company and buy it together.

This is the way that I bought the site with Tony in Leeds. I suggested he do it in his name, but he wanted to feel like we were officially partners. It really makes no odds to me, as long as I am getting paid.

It is imperative to speak to your own solicitor and accountant before ever entering into a joint venture. Even though Tony is a very close friend, I still persuaded him to have his own solicitor and be legally represented. This is good practice and saves any unforeseen circumstances or misunderstandings down the line.

If anybody asks you for money but tries to prevent you from speaking to your own solicitor, that is a major red flag. You do not have to take your solicitor's advice, but they will have your back, and they will spell out the risks of each and every deal or partnership you enter into.

<u>Seeing the Development to Completion</u>

Having a good power team is essential for this. I am very fortunate to have Ben overseeing all our projects. You should never scrimp on your professional fees because they will make or break a project. Never cut corners or go for the cheapest because you end up getting exactly what you pay for. Depending on the site, you will need a recommended and experienced planning consultant, architect, structural engineer, quantity surveyor and of course a good building team.

Once the development is complete you should have a good estate agent in place to sell the properties. Never go with a cheap agent and never put tenants in new-build properties that you intend to sell, or they will instantly lose their premium value.

It can be very effective to market your new-builds prior to them being built with the right Computer-Generated Images and guidance from a good agent. Some agents will advise to start your price listing high and then come down if they struggle to sell. However, this sends a bad message and you do not want a bunch of new builds sticking. Other agents will advise starting low to encourage interest, but this is also bad advice in my opinion. When selling lots of houses in one go I usually recommend listing them for the actual market value to begin with. Once you have sold the majority you can always use those clever marketing tricks to shift the last one or two.

Exit strategies also play a crucial part of any development project. What if you cannot get planning permission, finance or even sell them at the end of the project?

You need to have a Plan B that will not leave you

financially crippled in the worst-case scenario.

Every project comes with some level of risk, that is the nature of all business. Usually the higher the risk, the greater potential for a high reward.

We did not manage to sell our Lincoln new-builds as quickly as we hoped. Some sold immediately, but we decided to refinance some of the others. It was a perfectly good Plan B.

If you can not get planning permission, then at worst you might have to just sell it to a land banker or just to someone at auction. If you did not pay over the odds you probably will not lose that much. Be prepared for the worst-case scenario.

If you do manage to get planning permission but have not got the resources or funds to carry out the build, you can probably just sell and profit from the planning game.

Do not invest what you can not afford to lose and always have exit strategies for every deal.

If you educate yourself, you will most likely make good money on most of your projects. You might lose money on a few but should also make enormous amounts on a few too.

The key is to set a game plan and get the right people in place around you. Remember if you fail to plan, you plan to fail.

At the time of writing, I have more than £100,000,000 worth of developments in the pipeline, and another £10,000,000 worth being developed. My plan is to become a billionaire, but more importantly to help a lot of people, make the world a better place and keep on doing what needs to be done.

Exact Next Steps to Get Started

Five small action points that you must do before finishing this book:

1. Right now, without any procrastinations, book a free ticket to the Property Development Secrets Live - www.property-investors.co.uk/development which is the UK's No.1 training course on property development and also a great opportunity for you to meet and network with other likeminded people.

2. Connect with three property developers on social media and drop them a message informing them that you are getting started. You never know they might have some deals for you. Don't be shy, winners love to network. You can even start by messaging me on instagram.

3. If you are an accredited investor or a high net worth individual, take a look at my current development deals on www.leedsventures.com and consider doing a joint venture with your first deal.

4. Write down some big goals that scare you, then share them with a friend. When you speak things out, you speak them into existence.

5. If you enjoyed this book, please do leave me a review on Amazon and help spread the word to help others get started in their property development journey.

Thank you so much for taking the time to read this concise book. I cannot wait to meet you in person and I sincerely hope to see you become a wildly successful property developer.

Email : team@property-investors.co.uk

Redeem Your FREE Tickets

Either scan the QR code

The Secrets Of Property Development Live
by Samuel Leeds

Redeem Your FREE Ticket Here

Or visit:
www.property-investors.co.uk/development

Printed in Great Britain
by Amazon